CASPAR HAUSER

CASPAR HAUSER

A POEM IN
NINE CANTOS BY
DAVID CONSTANTINE

BLOODAXE BOOKS

ISBN: 1 85224 299 X

First published 1994 by
Bloodaxe Books Ltd,
P.O. Box 1SN,
Newcastle upon Tyne NE99 1SN.

Bloodaxe Books Ltd acknowledges
the financial assistance of Northern Arts.

ACKNOWLEDGEMENTS

This poem was first published, in instalments,
in *PN Review*. An abbreviated version of the poem was
broadcast on BBC Radio 3 in 1994, and parts were read on
Radio 4 by Marina Warner in her 1994 Reith Lectures.

Cover printing by J. Thomson Colour Printers Ltd, Glasgow.

Printed in Great Britain by
Bell & Bain Limited, Glasgow, Scotland.

'Where the devil should he learn our language?'
THE TEMPEST, II.ii.

CONTENTS

NOTE

The facts of Caspar Hauser's story which matter for my poem are as follows. Incarcerated for most of his childhood and adolescence he appeared in Nuremberg at Whitsuntide 1828, able to write his name and say, without understanding it, one sentence: *I want to be a rider like my father was.* The city fathers put him into the charge of a retired schoolteacher called Georg Friedrich Daumer, and it was in Daumer's house, in October 1829, that an unknown assailant struck him across the forehead with a heavy razor. Daumer, an invalid, soon afterwards asked to be relieved of the responsibility of looking after him, and Caspar moved in with Clara and Johann Christian Biberbach – but only for a few months. Clara conceived a passion for him, which he did not reciprocate, and he was moved into the safer keeping of Gottlieb von Tucher, still in Nuremberg. Then the eccentric Lord Stanhope appeared on the scene and made Caspar his ward, removing him to the town of Ansbach in December 1831 and lodging him with another schoolmaster, one less humane than Daumer, a man by the name of Johann Georg Meyer. Stanhope himself, having shown great fondness for the boy, went travelling, and after January 1832 never saw him again. Caspar was murdered just before Christmas 1833. He went to meet a stranger at a monument in the the public park in Ansbach. He seems to have hoped that at this meeting the truth about his life would be revealed. But the stranger stabbed him. Why he was confined, let out, assaulted, murdered, has never been quite explained. Probably, as the jurist Anselm von Feuerbach believed, he had a claim to the throne of Baden; but because of his innocence and the extraordinary reactions of his untried nervous system to a life in the daylight people at once invested more than a dynastic, political, worldly interest in him. He was an enigma, and excited all kinds of hopes and longings.

In German there is a vast literature on Caspar Hauser. I have read a good deal of it, but experts will soon see that I have taken many liberties in the pursuit of my own conception of the subject.

In six of the nine cantos I imagine Daumer, Clara Biberbach and Lord Stanhope, each near death, reflecting on their dealings with Caspar.

First Canto

Whit Monday 1828 he stood
In Nuremberg in the biggest empty square
Bang in the middle of it where

They burned people and broke them on the wheel
And showed their hearts and bowels to other people.
He stood there swaying on his sticky feet,

His head was bowed, the light had hurt his eyes,
The pigeons ran between his feet like toys
And he was mithered by the scissoring swifts,

Their screams and shadows, then the hour
Rolled off an iron tongue in an iron tower
And clouted him, like ferrets sound

Screwed the discovered burrows of his ears
And through the cobblestones
Another massive novelty of pains

Entered his fork. Even an embryo
Raises its little paws against the din
But Caspar stood there sucking it all in,

Dowsing for more of it on the square's navel,
Arms stiff like compasses, at the end of one
He held his letter of introduction

'To whom it may concern' and at the end
Of the other a wide-awake hat,
Both very tightly. There he remained

Just as the man behind him had set him up
On a morning of primary colours in the time
Between the moonlit and the sunlit crimes

In the town's arena, wept and wetted himself
And felt the blood in his boots, until the windows
Folded their wooden lids back and in rows

Diminishing to points under the eaves
From all the openings of their ordinary lives
The people stared at their accustomed space

Larger, as it seemed, and quieter and emptier
And all their beams were gathered at the centre
As by a heavy ore, or by a vacuum.

Caspar was tugging them. Down the stairways
And down the alleys of their daily bread
Blind as a mole he drew them by the eyes

Singly, hand in hand, in families,
Lifting the children up and shoving gently like
The beasts towards Adam, towards this stake,

This tree, this thing blown in by Pentecost,
They inched, already aghast
At all the questions he would make them ask.

II

Perhaps in a pitch black he would have been spared it
But there were eyes on him, the outside
Dimly through the nailed lids peered in

Down the length of him from beyond
Where his particular self came to an end
And in a darkness riddled with motes of light

He sprouted, whitish, his faint soles
Slowly, slowly, pushing towards a daylight
Only a shade more white than midnight

And even at noon never cruel. In time
The timbre of his grunts deepened
And curly dark hairs came up around

The ignorant staff of his sex. His pulses ticked,
But time for Caspar was as Luther guessed
It might be for God: all in a heap, at rest.

His repeated wakings did not seem to advance him
Only brought water, every time he woke
There was the water he loved in a clay beaker

And a clod of bread speckled with carraway seed.
He believed he slept these necessaries to his right side
Handy by, he ate, he drank, he fed

And watered the little horses, he dressed them,
So that it was a pleasure on his eyes,
With blue and red ribbons, and how they raced then

To and fro on their wheels at the end of his arm,
Their colours fluttering, an electricity went
All through him from the happiness of the movement.

The exhausted bread pushed through his coils meanwhile
At a certain pace, nosing like a mole
For its own moment of exit. Then he slid

Left over a hole and let it go through breeches
Cut out behind. Suddenly his sleepiness
Reaching a certain level tilted him backwards.

Everyone said there must be more to him, more time
Than the small space he recalled
When left and right he could touch the two cold walls,

More below that, at least the usual
Pit of years. I know a well
On an island where the clear fresh water rests

On the salt and lifts with it. Like that lay
Under Caspar's thin memory
An ocean in which most of him had sunk.

III

Right, the precipitates of sleep:
The bread and the water. Left, his sunken pot.
And left and right when he laid himself out flat

And sent his fingertips as far as they would go,
Two walls. A daylight faced him
Dimmer than the shell of the full moon on blue.

That was his room. If there was a ceiling
It never bothered him nor he it.
He slept between his little horses like a king.

Events came from behind. Waking, he rose
By a force, there was a hot wind on his nape
And like a stocks a wood lay across his knees.

He saw his hand, the playmate of his horses,
Under another of its kind, not his,
That clambered on it like a crab and fitted

A hard stick in and made queer jabs
And slides and slippy loops and when it stopped
Writing had come over the desk top.

It did it more, again and again and again,
Until the knowledge had taken
And Caspar's fist could move without a rider.

Those were his first steps on a white sheet,
Clutches of wriggling letters in black lead
Like tracks of worms on the Precambrian mud.

Sleeps came and went. Along with the bread and water
They flew in sharpened pencils and white paper.
He practised hard. Then he was overshadowed

Again by the hand. Riding his own
It pressed one of the little horses down
Hard on his writing and a pair of lips

In at the hairy opening of his ear
Down the quaint passageway
Again and again on pulses of warm air

Spat the one syllable, the hand
Working the plaything under Caspar's hand
To and fro, to and fro,

Until the name had come up through its wheels
And down the flex of Caspar's arm and muscles
And speech and writing touched their fingertips

In the horse's wooden body. Later he had
Sounds for himself like that, force-fed,
Trodden like a goose. The ghost hand

Busily applied them to him everywhere,
Belly and heart, mouth, eyes and hair,
It set the letters on his sunless clay,

Even drew up the cold balls of his feet,
Even went out to the limits of his reach,
To show how far his name was meant to stretch.

IV

Why then? With hindsight
We see the lessons were to equip him for life.
'Horse', he could say, and 'Caspar Hauser' and write

All three. But why, why start him ever,
Ever shunt him out of his silent shed
Into the traffic, who decided?

And then, what is this 'then'?
Suddenly the dust, the living grains of him
Are dumped in a hopper and begin to run

And the quiet heap of time is undermined,
Gravity riddles it, it begins to slide.
Then is when our clocks start, the hurrying kind.

Somebody shoves him off, he drifts, he sets,
He goes away faster and faster towards the falls.
Somebody connected him. Why then? Why at all?

When I dressed my son from behind, leaning over
Like a cosy sky, like a safe house, easing on
His cheerful leggings, socks, and smallest size in

Soft boots, I remembered gratefully
That I was warmed like this and had my back covered
And things done for me with a sweet silly commentary

Close in my ear. But Caspar woke on the dirt,
Stark, the hands were yanking breeches up him
With a bum for once, and boots that hurt.

He flopped like a mongol being dressed,
He was as slack as a collapsed marionette,
A giant one that has lain in its box and grown,

And against his delivery into the lives we lead
He offered the passive resistance of a corpse
Dragged out by a muffled man towards a cartload,

Or of a protester at a sit-in against the War
Gone heavy in the arms of the Law,
The hands making a buckle on his chest.

His underworld had steps and reaching these,
Arranging him on the third like a man of sorrows,
His keeper came at him on hands and knees

As if in obeisance or like
A fireman getting in under the smoke
And folded him over his shoulder upside down,

His nose on the itchy jacket,
And humped him up, up, a long climb,
Frequently resting, against the pull of home,

Against the needful love of the little horses.
He was a heavy earth. Dug out, he groaned
For his abandoned shape under the ground.

Divers need time, they need to come up slowly,
And Caspar needed months on every step
To harden. He was hurried. Only

The night-time was a mercy, on his eyes,
The colours sleeping, light at its quietest,
A bearable visibility. The rest,

All the waiting world, all the backed-up years,
As though he bled, as though through all his pores
He called for torture, when what little film

He wore was blown away, this all
Assembled like piranhas. He was the hole
Nature has a horror of, the greed, the thirst

Dug in her body, so the universe
Fell to filling him in. The winded man
Wheezing behind him like a buggered engine

Held him vertical on spaced feet
And the first rip-tides of nausea travelled him
Over the brew and fumes of a sweet May night

And terror when his flinching soles divined
The nervousness and hunger underground,
And he felt the moths on the dipped lamp of his face

And when he heard the winds of the stratosphere
In the hurtling planet's bright delighted hair.
Hung over chaos by the scruff he made

His three shaped sounds. 'Caspar', he said,
And 'Horse' and 'Hauser', but it did no good.
He felt like ants in a stabbed and burgled hill.

Then the march began. It began like this:
The man behind him pressed his thigh on his
And strode, the right, the left, the right, the left,

Holding him slumped. Anyone who ever
Rode on his father's shoes and took giant steps
Worked by his greater legs will have an idea,

A kind one. But the knack of it or the need
Lapsed out of Caspar after every stride
Until the man behind him kicked his heel

And the leg remembered. So towards Nuremberg
Little by little Caspar's feet were booted
And all the way the man behind him repeated

His third lesson, in at his heels it went
To the rhythm of their stiff trudging
In at his ear, a long statement:

I want to be a rider like my father was.
I want – kick – to be – kick – a rider – kick
Like my father was – kick, kick,

Caspar weeping. Thirty yards or so
In inches was as far as he could go.
Then the man behind him let him down to sleep.

So many sleeps he had on the way to Nuremberg
Face down on the heaving black-green earth,
So many hangovers, his poor head stupid

From the fragrances. Waking the first time
He met with the brutality of plain daylight:
Blinked, the world watered, everything went white.

Days in a white-out; even the night-time
Though it eased his eyes it put on perfume
Like a woman coming to bed; rain fell

Out of a sky he did not know existed
And water came to his mouth at the end of an arm
And fists of carraway bread.

Pairs before them have stumbled through the spring.
There was Antigone and the blind king,
Also the little girl and her blind minotaur

But Caspar never had a hand in his
Only on his neck and when the darkness
Would have allowed it he never saw a face

And when he sagged he kissed another patch of grass
And when he rose all his encouragement,
Spat in his ear, kicked in his heels, was

The difficult long sentence which he spoke
In pieces in a muddle with his name
And the sound for a horse and always meant the same:

Lay me down, make the pain less,
Sheath me in the dark again with the ribboned horses,
Only let me be. Instead

Head down against the birdsong and the scents
He barged his boots through flowers and the dried
Blood of the last stage in them liquefied.

One daybreak then, dewy themselves, they bowed
Their faces over the city of Nuremberg,
The light still kind, the squares, the houses showed

Gently through a veil. Hung by the neck, his lessons
Rattling faster and faster off his tongue,
He tumbled down to meet the citizens.

Second Canto

GEORG FRIEDRICH DAUMER
1 January 1875

I

Born in the spring of the century's first year
Lately the big questions have seemed to him answerable.
Where were we going after all? Answer:

Head down into the Age of Iron.
And thereafter? Nowhere. Iron is the last.
Or maybe lead. Some days it has that taste.

Iron or lead. Lead in the souls (the souls?)
Of such as us, the poets and the scholars,
Iron in the fists of those who govern us.

I should have been born in 1770
With Beethoven, Wordsworth, Hegel, Hölderlin,
I might have gone to Paris at the age of nineteen.

I should have moved to the centre.
Goethe would have welcomed me, I might have read
My Hafiz to him, but by then he was dead.

I am as old as the century.
I might have gone to Paris at the age of thirty
(Heine did) and in '48

I could have been in the *Paulskirche*.
There was never any shortage of barricades
I might have been on. Deeds,

However, were not his forte and look where
What was has got him, the reading and writing – here:
Loneliness, penury, a sad end

Among the poor who were always poor,
Poorer than they, they address him
As what he has been for fifty years: Professor,

Courteously, and leave him a cabbage on the step
Or a couple of billets of split wood or best of all
Half a bucket of slack brown coal.

Truth is, he has begun burning his library
Tome by tome in a strict order
Of greatest to less inefficacy.

The Bible first, a large one, he began with Revelations
Then back to Genesis. In twists with little cakes
Of wetted coal dust and the week's

Dried rinds it warmed some of the air and the side of him
Next the stove. The vellum Rosicrucians
He fed in like brickettes, transmuting them

Into heat and smuts.
The smuts continued falling on his head and hands.
Snow likewise on the streets.

Last to burn – he is as vain as the rest of us –
Will be the four dozen volumes of his published works
And first of them his *Cry of a Convert* which was

Of his innumerable wrong roads
The wrongest. He is saving
His three books on Caspar and the twelve boxes of notes

Till last, and prays (prays!)
He will die in a warmish interlude before next winter
And spare that fuel. For what? Who knows!

He saw Caspar again the other night
In the pitch black, white
And pointing at the wound in his side

So that the teacher come to the last dead end
Muddles his own and Caspar's peace of mind
Feels neither teacher nor pupil will ever rest

And burning books in the worst street in Nuremberg
Under their fall-out as the stove gives up
Its ghost of a warmth and his dewdrops drop

From a little height on to the old words
And on to the new ones written big on flattened shop-paper
He ponders for the last time over Caspar

Over his being, his origins, his innocence,
That above all – his innocence – but the truth
Seems to have lain a million years beneath

The dripping accretions which are
The writing of doctors, prelates and legal men
And of Professor Daumer again and again and again

Who to the bitter end cannot desist
But tortures the experience he indisputably had
After the meaning he feels he may have missed.

II

My good and learned friend
The jurist Anselm Feuerbach whom they poisoned
At Whitsun in the year

They stabbed poor Caspar during Advent
Laid on the grounds of his peculiar wrongs
The definition of a new capital offence:

The murder of a childhood, but the victim
Only felt pity for the man who had done that to him,
And wept to imagine the anxiety

Of a man jailing a child of his own kind
Twelve years in the dark, he said
He would not like to inhabit that man's mind

For it must be a dark place with nothing in it
Except the wrong that was growing by the minute
Bigger and bigger in a place that could not grow

Because its walls were the walls of a grown man's skull.
Later – and I can tell you precisely when –
It was the night of 1st August, we were in my garden

On the riverside, near my white statue
Which has gone now and with it the garden and my house
And what has been done to the river I will not tell you

But we were in my garden, Caspar and I,
More than two months after his appearance above ground
When I lifted up his face and he saw the starry sky.

There were showers of gold that night and the usual stars
Seemed nearer and many we had never seen
Were pressing down at us between

The black interstices and even I
Given the vision of his eyes
Felt the nearing of beauty like a booming noise

And shook at it, his heavy head
Lay back in the hollow of my hand and starlight filled
The vast pools of his face until they overspilled.

He lay collapsed across my lap
And such a weeping came up in him as though
He were a fountain for the whole earth's sorrow

And bitterness, and yet he could not bear
To wish on the man who had cut his starry nights
By thousands the forfeit of more

Than one. Later he grew
More into our way of looking at these things
But I will remember him when he was new

During the time when I had him in my house
And before I induced him to eat meat
For then his compassion was infinite.

I had him from our gaol where they had taught him
Fire is hot with a candle flame
And where he had set his fleas at liberty

One by one through the window bars
And the inrush of everything had almost killed him.
At twenty-eight I was already an invalid

With a few private pupils, living on the island.
My mother and sister kept house.
There in the river's arms we had some peace

And Caspar mended, a little, it was never enough,
For where can you walk in an average town like ours?
Nowhere, the public squares

Reek, every domicile
Does its own butchery, a hare hangs
Bleeding brilliantly at the nostril

From the fist of a woman gossiping in the sun.
Cooped, trussed, flayed, Creation
Emits only a little of its rightful scream.

Caspar heard the rest. Worse still
Even a wooden depiction pierced him like the real thing,
All those Christs, for example, hanging

From nails, in silence, with open mouths,
He asked why they must be perpetually tormented
And never cradled in our arms and tended.

I had begun to view the world as he did
And remembered watching my playfellows
Pin back a thrush's wings on the door of the shed

And spit her pimpled babes, to roast them.
I had begun to flinch as though there were blood
On every hand I shook and wherever I trod.

III

If the cold endures or the charity of the neighbours fails
And Professor Daumer begins to feed his stove
His own children, his titles,

Though he will preserve his Hauseriana to the bitter end
Last before them will be his efforts in rhyme,
His effusions to Zoroastra, to Womankind,

Nature, the Nine Virtues, the Four Last Things,
The East, the West, the Orphic Mysteries,
And his versions of Hafiz

And the English Lake Poets. He was noticed
Favourably more than once and Brahms released
A handful from prison in the century

By lending them music. Yesterday he addressed
Caspar's slandered shade
In seventeen quatrains no worse than all the rest.

Was Caspar Orpheus? On 4th April 1829
He greeted the beginnings of a new life
In forty-seven lines that rhymed

In nice writing and he might pen
Something on Duty, Friendship, Virtue, Fate
For a lady's album now and then.

But no, it never looked likely he would grow to be
As good as Professor Daumer at poetry.
Nor could he sing. And yet…One morning

In the first summer of his six above the surface
Caroline Daumer was playing Schubert in the garden room
When Caspar appeared, like a ghost, she said, his face

Was shining like a hill with streams,
His fists were clenched, his forearms crossed
Like cross-bones hard against his breast

And he said: 'It feels him strongly here'
And that the sadness in him was enough already
Without the music making it any more.

He felt he was saying goodbye to the shape he had.
The music unravelled him and he was sad
To be coming loose so soon

Never having set into anything definite
Never having made himself at home under his name
Always unsure where he and the outside met

Where his own writ ran. His ears, for example,
He was only led to discover by our gaoler's son
Who took his finger and thumb and pinced the lobe of one,

The nose likewise and conned
Over the bumpy braille of a face with its own hand.
But shown the lot in a glass still nothing clicked.

Pain, in his feet, say, caused him to realise
He owned extremities, but not who this 'he' was
Nor where it lived. When our phrenologist

Took Caspar's head in his long cold hands
Poor Caspar begged him not to unfasten it.
Everything threatened to quit,

The heart pulled like a learner and receiving music
Almost shut down. It troubled Daumer
That Caspar never made the first person stick.

However often corrected he would edge
Out again and again into the third
Like a man on a window ledge

Outside himself. That summer
Once he was on the mend Professor Daumer
And Dr Osterhausen put him to the minerals

At the index finger of his right hand
And measured the shock. Lead hit the elbow,
Iron the shoulder, diamond

Via the eyes (they spouted) drove
As far as the pit below the heart. Degrees
Of cold, distances travelled, intensities

Felt of cold, out of the infinite
Waiting cold of the earth through the little ambassadors
Gathered in Professor Daumer's cabinet,

Gold, silver, platinum, mercury and malachite,
Amber and amethyst, copper and zinc were let
Into Caspar's side, the right,

For the left conducted without the least resistance
And shock after shock of cold to the heart's pit
They dared not risk it.

A crystal glass released
From the corners of his mouth and the centre of his lower lip
Three icy lines that fused

In the throat, and sank. And this
That he was chased through and through with veins,
Courses and capillaries

That sucked like vampires at all the holes and tits
Of the earth's cold matrix fits
Caspar for the fraternity of Orpheus who are

Much too open and fray like spume
And dance in the warm sun – or the cold moon-beam
Equally gaily, like dead dust or genes.

He was too long in the ground, no wonder
He could smell the dead who are there for longer
Like a seam of coal. He said the mouths

Even of the lustiest were draughty. His spine
Felt like a column of mercury
If Professor Daumer fifty yards behind

Wagged a finger at it. Horses too
He said blew cold at him. He sat as though
A magnet in the earth had found him through

The shoes, the stirrups, the iron in the saddle frame,
So that the one sentence dinned into his ear
That what he wanted was to be a rider

Must pull him back again to the little horses
He had been buried with. Though horses stand
Plumb in the sun, four square, and lend

A shape of the air more bodily warmth than we do
They tap the cold of the earth as Caspar did,
It springs up where they tread

So cold it hurts the throat. And this was true
Even of Pegasus who kicked off and flew.
Caspar had a large red roan. She shone

Like those under the Pyrenees that shine
In a sort of upper room
Above the pit, only when the torches come.

IV

To the pure water he loved
At the end of August I added a first drop
Of beef tea. Since he had caught us up

In many things by then: could do
Long multiplication and long division,
Wrote a fair hand, drew

Heads, fruit and flowers nicely
And played a piece of Schubert tolerably well
I thought him ready for meat. He could smell

The cling of it on a white bone
At ten paces and my one drop in his full stein
Caused him to sweat, shake, weep and vomit

But I hardened him drop by drop and then
With fibres as fine as the stigmas of saffron
Until his appetite was redder then mine.

He wore a top hat when he rode out.
I began him on Latin and the preachers
Were sidling as near as they dared, like vultures.

His stools which had been as regular as clockwork
And as sweet as a horse's shifted uneasily
And stank. Sad to say

Our savage cat who would come to nobody but him
And sought him in the garden with a length of coloured ribbon
And they played for hours, it was a joy to watch them,

She smelled the change, and left him. In spring
We put him to the metals again.
None mounted him as it had done:

Lead to the wrist, iron to the elbow,
Diamond to the shoulder. Even his left side now
Took them up bearably. But that same day

He composed his first verses: on the new life
Opening before him, as it seemed, and mine too,
My life, my verses, at last came true,

I thought, as I busied myself
With the marvellous boy while the light still
Lasted around his head, before night fell.

Caspar the fading coal, the Way that led
Or would have led down Daumer's cellar steps
To the Mothers perhaps

Into the zone of the EN KAI PAN
Where everything moves and flows and man
Enters the round of the angels and the animals.

There was more of this. For even as Caspar's soles
And palms hardened and he put on weight
And the light went off him as off a landed rainbow trout

Daumer consulting his faeces
Monitoring the performance of his six senses
Logging his speech, his thoughts, his dreams

As he showed him in various circles
There occurred, he said, a leaching of virtue,
A transmission of zest into himself, the minder, who

Until then had only moped in life. He wrote:
I stopped shielding my eyes. I saw the radiance
Of a life everlasting in the near distance.

He meant it figuratively, of course. The eyes
In his head watered as usual and he shielded them
And perhaps the lasting life he saw was only fame

As the curator of a freak,
His archivist. Or – Daumer again – more like
His disciple, his priest. He would have been

My psychopomp and let me into the first circle
At the strait gate from where the circles slant
And spiral one below the other in a long descent.

Even on the threshold I began to sing
Even going in and down only a little way.
Kairos, the moment, it was my opportunity.

V

Poor Daumer. He was reckoning without
Terror. He knew from literature
That where the tight earth split

At Delphi, say, or Cuma, the truth was cold
And anyone drinking it was riddled with shock for days
And floes of it jostled

Among the corpuscles thereafter
Never quite melting. Did he suppose
It would be warmer in his reasonable house,

Mother there, a sister playing Schubert,
A title before his name, the century
Getting on nicely into modern times? In May

Caspar drew the head of an ambiguous angel
And dreamed in every detail
A palatial home: the flights, the suites,

The mirrors and statues. In Caspar's copperplate
Daumer gave a version to the newspapers
Under the epigraph (translated)

'Clouds of Glory'. Seen again
The angel had a smile about as friendly
As the flayer Apollo's. Daumer's garden,

Allowed a measure of self-expression in the English style,
Let rip with poppies as though an old wound
That night had suddenly opened

In a fit of weeping. Indoors
Caspar drew little arrangements of quieter flowers
For ladies' keepsakes. So far as the sun knew

And the blazing stars he was a year old.
Like everyone else he meant to make a decent score.
Soon he was not much odder than foreigners always are.

Everyone liked him: his courtesy, the way
He pieced together what he had to say
Before he delivered it, making a ring meanwhile

Of his thumb and index finger and splaying
The others out hard. He had an honest face,
A striver's, a washed and brushed-up ploughboy's,

And shone goodnaturedly in his Sunday clothes.
Everyone said he was doing very well,
Better than Bishop Fricke's negro, for example,

Or Lady Amalia's Huron Indian. Neither lived.
He fainted less and ate
Even sweetbreads. Swifts and swallows arrived

And nightingales sang in Daumer's garden
On the lovely continuo of the parted river.
Soft days, a mild sky, lessons in the open air

Near the Cnidian and against the darkness
Over our quiet suppers or a game of chess
We shone like tableaux. Then one morning

Mother went in to him: nothing belonged, the room
Looked to have lost what ever made it home
And he had backed into a far corner

Behind the ramparts of his knees and arms
Very small except his eyes
Which begged her. We were days

Reasoning with him: his colossal strides,
His vaster hopes, our greater and greater love and last,
Gently as we could, his duty. He complied

And bowed himself once more to the timetable
But always as though he were cold across the shoulders,
He looked in mirrors often, he seemed unable

To leave the back of his skull alone. It meant
He had lost the dispute with his visitant
And the heart in him was swapped for a source of dread.

So I suppose. He must have suffered
Proof such as music is
Or falling in love but to the contrary and stared

Life in the face until her eyes,
So beautiful that summer, opened
Like old shafts and joined

The nose and mouth. We were gentle with him,
Nobody called but friends and when, as always,
We let the children in to climb the cherry trees

He was the one they honoured with the bowl,
The cherry bowl that has that name all year
In waiting for the renewal

Of its wood by fruit, and when the pirates set
Their head of cherries on the table where he sat
Like an orphaned king, I saw his hands,

Opening round the appearance in quick belief,
Suddenly disciplined as though to say
This may be real but why show it me?

His present, the little bridgehead
He had made on life, by now
Had entered the shadow of a lifted

Weapon so that he shivered on the warmest day
And through our company
Peered like a marked man through his bodyguard

And this, being looked through, being looked behind,
Serving as taster on the gifts of summer,
Having to weight the words of life with more and more

Conviction, wore the Professor down.
Mother laid the orphan in her widowed lap
And sang the old spells in an undertone

All the while working with her fingers at his haunted skull,
But Daumer monitoring the more or less of sadness,
The more or less of anxiety dressed

Every morning with an effort, spoke with care
As though his voice would crack, and seeing the core
Of the cherry tree abruptly evacuate

A pack of crows and the unscared
Rats retreat with an insolent slowness
Down the cellar steps he felt his life had queered.

Autumn was beautiful. The conkers shone like cherries
And the leaves amazed us by their size
Like hands descended from a pediment

And with the willow leaves they yellowed over
The pitch-black water in the backs.
Blue days, never any hurry, the smoulder

And flare of fires, a whiff of mist.
He followed me everywhere like my living shadow,
My shade, I had almost said, my chilly ghost,

And I braced him less than a teacher should,
The encouragements went rotten in my mouth.
The fear had become so strong, a mould

Of it followed us wherever we went
Like faith, that in the air
Once made a space for the white unicorn to appear.

Thanksgiving. Even now I love the festivals.
Gratitude is as much our mark as grief.
I love God's house, the barn of our collected souls,

When it fills with thanks, I sidle in
For the birth, the resurrection and the harvest.
I think I love the festival of autumn best:

The crammed ark on the brink of another winter,
Every space and ledge is heaped with stores,
The windows lighted bravely with asters,

We know the perils, we sink or swim together,
We pool the innocent produce of our hands,
And cast ourselves upon the mercy of the weather.

We minded Caspar in the family pew
Behind four walls in a singing congregation
But it did no good. He could not sing. He knew

The fearful vacancy was filled,
I felt him trembling against me when we kneeled,
Heard him plead. No good. The angel came,

And chivved him. The Saturday
Waking he sweated, froze, clutched at a pain in the abdomen
And accompanied Caroline to market. When

She stood he tugged at her skirt like a two-year old
For the travelling atoms of his fear reassembled
Behind him while she gossiped.

Because of his sweats and frosts
I excused him a mathematics lesson with Dr Wenders
And carried another book of mine to the printers.

Mother was in, and Caroline, also the servant girl.
I consult his own account. At eleven he answered a call
Of nature in the privy in the hall.

Finished, he was considering how to describe it
For my records, when the house-bell sounded very lightly.
He rose, buttoning himself in the friendly darkness

And opened the privy door. His fear stood
Made visible with gloves and bandages like the invisible man
And played a measured backhand across his forehead

With a heavy razor. That was that.
Over the eaves of his eyebrows a downpour of blood.
He whimpered, crumpled, lay in the wet.

Waking, he seemed to wish to slobber everything:
The flags, the stairs, the banisters, the landing,
All my house and home. He sullied books

Lent him for learning in his room on the first floor,
He blundered like an escapee from an abattoir,
His prints were everywhere, his drops exploded on the boards.

He wanted Mother. She was on the second floor.
Blinded, dumb with the blood, in such a bewilderment
When I remember that he went

Down, not up, down all the slippery stairs
And raised the cellar trap, making for the dark, and I remember
The rats in there and how the water from the river

Seeped in and the big rats splashed in it,
This cold room where I sit
Thinking suddenly drops another degree or two

In terror, which I note
With satisfaction as an evidence of being,
Or having been, alive. I met

The women where the puzzling blood had brought them
At the open hole, found him
By candle on the far side of the water.

It was hard to uncurl the child again
For of all our pleasant house, of all its sunny rooms
With views of spires, trees, white clouds sailing, none

Suited him now like the cellar for it most
Resembled the pit he grew in and where his fear was least.
He masked his face against my candle with his hands

And through his leaky fingers he seemed to be weeping blood.
He was as red as a savage when he lay revealed,
Drenched, and as loose in all his limbs as a man on the wheel.

VI

We gave him a new room, whitewashed,
And a few late flowers. Sitting up bandaged
And making the sign of the circle with his left hand

He spoke an account of what had happened to him.
I took it down verbatim
Like scripture, like the Word

Sprung, unhusked, shining for the first time in our vernacular.
When his own hand was strong enough he did me a copy out fair,
Illuminating it with asters and candles.

Now all his gifts were upon him again
As in the days before he ate flesh.
Seizing the hour I alerted Dr Osterhausen

And very gently we put him to the ordeal of the metals.
He took them up his blood as though electrified
And we were obliged to spare his left side.

Visitors came, across the two bridges,
The police, the church, our dignitaries,
And the common people queued like the people of Bethany.

I let them in in threes and they stood at a distance
Making a dumbshow of condolence
And everybody felt a mite ashamed.

At the removal of his bandages
A painter should have been present, our visages
Were fit for history when we saw the mark

Of the cutting edge of the angel's wing across his brow.
It was an almost sightly disfigurement, far
Easier to look at than a duelling scar,

More like a line of thought. So for a while still,
Bled and delicate, in a white room and the lower floors
Scrubbed clean, he lived in my house until

My spirit, my nerve, my hold, whatever it is
We need or cannot speak, move,
Go about our business, converse with friends, love

Anyone, do anything
That helps, it left me, suddenly one early morning
Of rain, of black conclusive rain.

Poor man. He had soaped his face like Father Christmas,
Wetted his cut-throat and a voice whispered:
Why not draw a thin red smile with it from ear to ear?

Mother found him sitting in his shirt, still lathered.
He looked as old as her long-dead father.
The blade was folded near the copper bowl.

Questioned, he said he had had enough of everything:
Caspar, angels, the Mothers, blood on his books.
He was a scholar and an invalid, his shakes,

Runs, turns, were coming back again. A whining monotone,
Geriatric. He was twenty-nine.
He shut his poorly eyes and Mother shaved him.

Through the study window he could see the two policemen.
They had built a little lean-to and were quite at home
With a charcoal stove. They checked whoever came

At the point of a bayonet and anyone
Leaving with the ghostly Caspar had them tagging on
At just the right distance for a constant mockery.

The salutes they gave were clownish. Now and then
They fired off their muskets at a pigeon by way of a joke,
Frightening Caspar silly. For perhaps a week

Receiving the town in his little bedroom
He had seemed beyond fear, martyred and over it,
Soon we should have brought him the halt and the lame

And expected signs. Now he was animal again
And clung to Daumer as a cowardly Jesus
Might have to a fatherly Judas.

And the Professor peering ahead saw nothing but horrors:
His nice house darkened by Caspar and the jailers
And sapped by rats. He jumped if a door slammed,

Wept if the milk was late. Then bad reviews
Prostrated him behind a migraine for two days
And he listened to Caspar whimpering through the ceiling.

Mother, he said, see where I am with this trouble,
My eyes worse, not a thought in my head.
Will I ever put pen to paper again? He lay in bed

Turning his face to the proverbial wall
And heard a voice whisper
Deliver up Caspar and all will be back to normal,

The onus gone. He wanted to be let off.
Things as light as a drop of rain or a leaf
Weighed on him when they landed

But Caspar squatted on him like a nightmare
All of lead. Enough of the frontier,
Enough of heights and depths and having his dim eyes opened!

Professor Daumer wanted the golden mean again,
The little manageable *train-train*
On half pay, and his bowels in order.

Advent. There was a skull
In every little window Caspar opened. He could smell
Betrayal coming. Daumer had them

Padlock the cellar door. He lay sick.
Whenever Mother entered he was worse and worse.
Whose mother was she then? Of course

She took the hint and begged him to think of himself for once
And put himself first and his important work and put
Caspar on the Parish. He held out

All the while weeping with relief in the inner man
Until it was clear that it was *force majeure*,
Mother, he bowed to, a mother's love, and her

Fault, not his. Mother made me, he said,
To all and sundry in the years to come and yes, she repeated,
Until the day she died, I made him,

I fetched him pen and ink. That was the hardest
Writing he ever did, Professor Daumer used to say,
Though every 'i' was dotted, every 't' crossed

Already in his head. With regret
And expressions of gratitude for all he had done to date
The Elders accepted the Professor's resignation on health grounds

From onus for Caspar. The howl
When he was fetched. It clung
Like bats against the walls and ceiling.

Daumer covered his ears with another pillow.
He saw the attraction of a dark cellar,
He conceived a horror of his shaving mirror,

And opened books in dread
For on more pages than he remembered,
On more and more, as it seemed, Caspar had bled.

❦

Third Canto

CLARA BIBERBACH
24 May 1852

I

'Clara' I liked, and for an after-name
I took my mother's when I had gone from where
Behind my back they called me Mrs Potiphar

And Mrs Johann Christian Biberbach to my shameless face.
I ask you: Biberbach! He sealed
His deals with a beaver beavering away

Like him, day in day out, he left at six,
Came home at midnight, sex
He set aside ten minutes for

After evensong until I had a son
To carry on from him when he was gone
And then he stopped it. I was twenty-five.

I joined the Union of Charitable Mothers.
The Father when I said
I was having the bad thoughts in the early mornings said

Count your blessings, mostly wives confessed
All they wanted was eternal rest
From it, and I would keep my figure at least

Only having the two. For what? She tried
To age as little as possible after Caspar died
Since he could not. If she went home to die

At least they would concede she has worn well.
But she will be buried with her mother's people
As Mme Clara Citelle, a widow

Childless and respectable. In Nuremberg at fairs
Over her children's heads she watched the whores
Hooking soldiers, and her heart beat

Like the hooves of scandal getting close.
She lay in the early morning sleepy shallows
Elaborating pictures of herself

Masked and naked in a *maison de passe*
For a couple of captains.
She said: If it happens it happens

And put herself daily nearer to where
It might. Marry
And burn is the worst of both worlds. Standing there

One evening she was looked at like the girls
Straight in, and that was itself the fall
For after that she was sure every man could tell.

Her face allowed it. Sooner or later
Somebody calling would be bound to twig her.
It was a youngish gentleman from the comptoir

During the lassitude after lunch. Her hurry scared him,
He left dispirited but put the word about
She was a pushover. A lie. I made a note

Whenever it happened in my private diary
And but for that first week
When I was catching up as you might say

Once a month was the most and only then
If I couldn't help it. Johann Christian
Some Sunday evenings said I was looking well.

The hour reminded him but I made excuses
Nicely. He gave me money for dresses
Instead, and nodded off. So it continued

And I could live with it. I was never in love much
Before Caspar and generally what I saw
When the waves of it came on me were more and more

Lifting on the rim of infinity
And I wanted those too, I wanted them breaking in me
Down where some chap was rooting the best he could

And I stared over his shoulder
For a sight of heaven through our fancy ceiling.
Any woman would. It was my idea

To offer sanctuary to the Child of Europe.
I saw him in his little bedroom sitting up
Like Lazarus. The Professor was cool with me

And his mother sniffed. To be honest
I liked the idea of a police escort.
By that time – I was at my scarletest –

They were already saying he was a king's son
And God would justify him. Holding court
In a spotless shirt he looked like someone

Not like us. There was quite a crowd
Followed them dragging him off the island in the snow
And a man with his belongings in a wheelbarrow.

Upstairs, looking for them coming,
Clara suddenly opened the flimsy curtains on herself.
Gentlemen doffed their toppers, but for the moon-calf

Within a week she forsook them all.
Their cards collected on a platter in the hall
Like season tickets after expiry.

II

I felt like royalty myself when we walked out
Him on my arm and the six-foot
Fusiliers marching behind us.

We did the shops and took a stroll in the Nuns' Garden.
He wore a black fur hat, the first
Gift I gave him, so that he should look more foreign

As I desired it. My sable swept the snow.
Or we drove on the ramparts and had a view
Of tracks, villages, woodlands come out black

On the utter white. We rode there too.
He had a mare of a peculiar burning red
And fitted her, or she him, as Eve did

The gap in Adam. I ended jealous
That she had secrets with him. But all was
Novel in the early year, the town

I was sick of brightened and tasted savoury
When I dismissed his other teachers and we two
Wandered. Once in the ghetto

We met the Professor. He wore a plaid
Like an old man. He eyed
Our guard. I remember a beam of sunlight coming in,

A canary singing and the spiced air
Whispering Yiddish and I was proud of my adventure
With Caspar and prouder still

When the Professor asked did the blue devils
Plague him any the less and Caspar slid
My arm under his wing, so to speak, and said

The devils of every colour had flown away.
We were all deceived. I checked my gaiety
Enough not to call Professor Daumer Grandad.

He looked like Judas had he lived
To see Christ risen. An early Easter. My heart set
Finally on what it could do best:

Love Caspar. He loved her clothes,
Had Caroline's but Daumer corrected him.
At Biberbach's no fatherly friend protected him

And he fell to the woman. He loved her dresses,
The infinite work in each, the intricacies
Of fastening, the slips and loops, the minute markings

And the amplitude, like chestnut trees
In flower at Whitsun on a sunny breeze,
And scarves and veils and all her underthings

So soft and light and sheer.
He rose early, did some scripture
And simple book-keeping left him by Biberbach

But when the house was quiet, the children
Governed, he felt an attraction
Attack him through the floors, walls and doors

From Clara's clothes as she chose among them.
She chose slowly, expecting him.
He came and sat there like a dumb waiter

And she laid the day's things across his arms
In the order for putting on. One colour
Of love was running into the next in her,

A red. Ladies who dress
And undress in the expressionless
View of their black attendants

Were on her mind. April 3rd
She and her shivery image in the glass agreed
She had the same permission. Clara heard

The pretty tolling of his usual hour.
She turned to face him with a different look,
Counting ten. But the tenth stroke

Fell together with a pistol shot
A worse noise than the rooms of a house can bear
Or the ear's caves and corridors will ever forget.

Then in the damaged silence she heard a thing
Shouldering towards her through a labyrinth
Always thwarted, so that now it was nearer

And now cold again and she there at the centre
Could only sit, neither call out nor lift a hand
But only sit like the prize in a dream or legend

Somewhere unbearable for what might be delivery or murder
To slither and bawl closer. Her bedroom broke
Open on Caspar. He wore a hood and cloak

All of blood, he smeared and slopped
The day's light pastel pretty colours and stopped
His brute encumbered crown

Against her lap's
Deeper and deeper diaphanous soft shelter
And Clara mired her hands. The guard disburdened her.

It was an accident. He had furrowed
His head near the right eye. Biberbach showed
The ball to visitors, lodged in a beam,

Like the mark where Luther threw his inkhorn at the devil.
The Elders said he was wrong to leave a pistol
Handy where the unhappy Caspar

Bowed himself every morning to the study of God and Mammon.
Caspar said it was the angel's wing again.
Clara kept the négligée with its vast stain

In the lap and burned the rest.
The house resumed. She filled with haste
Seeing him marked twice across the brows

And ended his convalescence with the slow
Unclothing and slower clothing of her body before him.
He sat immobile like a dead pharaoh.

Morning after morning thus, the sun streaming in,
She stood so that it watered on her skin
And over the blackness of her shock of woman hair

And on her breasts' dark haloes. In silence then
Against her wishes she dressed from the tray
His arms made, and this was the sum of her sin,

Except once when I made him nuzzle me
And once, God forgive me, I felt whether
His thing was stiff, but only his arms ever were

And they held out like iron under my day's
Costume. Truth is
He liked me better dressed and when everything was on

He was as pestering as a puppy dog
And I sobbed inside, in there, in my womb
For him to be like other men and want the same.

It was the time of the first *vita*,
Riddled with errors, and the exaltation of him as Europe's Child
Or the Once and Future King. Daumer appealed

In the name of Virtue and the Sciences
For his removal into more appropriate circumstances.
And Clara beat her sunny nakedness

Day after day against him helplessly,
Against his smile, against his absent stare,
Like a moth that cannot flare

Only beat and beat. The pack meanwhile
Whom Caspar had ousted, wanting to be back in,
Dropped hints into the cuckold's ear his jewel

Of a lady might be in some peril
At home all day with Caliban. One morning,
A morning when everything was going wrong,

They saw him suddenly snap a pen and mess
His thin fastidious
White hands and leave hatless.

It was after ten. Clara sat
Hugging her left knee on the window seat,
Naked, receiving the sun and weeping quietly,

Caspar the clothes-horse distant. Clara says:
I took the lie he offered me, the lie
Everyone knew was one and not for his and not for my

Good name but to spite the clod
Caspar, my heart's sole want and hope, and to end
My hellish mornings. Johann Christian penned

An explanation to the Councillors who roared
With laughter but shifted the boy I could not look in the eye
Away. And then I whored,

I sobbed and howled under one after the other
Till his bed stank of it and he slept
Curled away from me like a cheese rind and crept

Off earlier and earlier. I saw him play
With the pistol but I sent
For a clerk from under his nose as one sends out for tea

And the butcher's boy, calling
With a little bloody package in his soft hands,
Climbed to the master's room and I received him kneeling.

Then stopped, it was over, my life there.
Husband, the necessary son, the unnecessary daughter
Looked at me blankly as from a family portrait

Done two hundred years ago and where I should have stood
I was painted out. Nobody touched me,
I was like a leper. Only Caspar saluted,

Passing to a lesson under guard, he bowed,
He would have come across to touch my glove,
But they hustled him on. He forgave

Or was ignorant of everything. Then came
The devil himself in the shape
Of Philip Stanhope,

An English lord, and of Caspar's blood, some lost
Already on Daumer's books and more running to waste
In Clara's disappointed lap, the rest

Which might have gone with hers
To make a little dynasty of innocence
Ran out at Christmas

Over the snow in the town of Ansbach
In a public park
And down the whited streets.

I broke my heart crying when I heard,
Abroad, incognita, I sat and stared
Like a nun at my brown relic,

Guilty. In my house
All the first week he had barred his frightened face
Against me with his fingers

But I loosened them and ceased
Being jealous of Caroline Daumer's hands
Playing on his for mine too phrased

Life differently, he said himself
That he was lifted up on the new year
As when a wind comes and we see the grey sky tear

And the blue that is always there above it spreads
Like certitude
And the high snows and the washed green fields are made

Visible quickly, all in a smaller time
Than it takes us to open our heavy clothes to it
And breathe again, seeing a road run straight

Somewhere elsewhere, somewhere not like here,
Among a different people, where we might have lived
Only a little oddly, I believed,

As man and wife, and the great houses,
The lawyers, the clergymen, the philosophers
Would have been as distant as another country's wars

And Caspar safe but he
Is dead long since and I soon shall be
And all I have of him is a patch of blood

And depths, depths that in between
His murdered childhood and his barely come of age
He sank in me. For I was shown

The way out of a life gone wrong and told
This is the only true
Way out and it is not for you.

That Whitsun everybody called the best
In living memory when they met
On the streets, especially where a street

Gave into any greenery
Entering the avenues and the parks, say,
And most where the colossal chestnut trees

Gored at the blue sky with their horns of plenty
The phrase 'in living memory'
Came on people's tongues again and again

Because of the scent, I suppose,
The wetted dust, the debris of blossom and the streaming seedpods
Because of the wind that was always tousling us

And lifting the unsettled strata of our years
And quickening the spores
That lie for example in the folds of dresses in a wardrobe

She woke feeling the day already flowing,
The body's atoms shivering,
Tears in the eyes, a desperation in the throat

Craving to melt, and Pentecost
Was borne upon her as the season of living memory,
The past obliged to dance, and the rest

Standing unwanted in the long mirror
Seeking to make her fingers meet around her waist
She saw it panic through the straits

Into the sump where all the grains
Are dead sand. Everything moved and flowed
But Caspar sat so that his shins, thighs, back, arms made

Exact rightangles and I laid out
For Whitsun of all my dresses the favourite,
Too girlish, I suppose, so light that in it

The breeze and I were wedded: that dress lay
Over the bars of Caspar's respectful arms
Like water, air, fire, or the corpse of me.

Fourth Canto

PHILIP HENRY STANHOPE
1 March 1855

I

Stanhope, Philip Henry, the Fourth Earl,
Dying abroad nowhere particular
I wish to be shipped home like an admiral

In brandy, I have a longing
To enter the mouth of the Thames on a flood tide
And settle alongside

Eleanor Mary, my poor wife, the children
Lawfully issued between her narrow hips,
Henry Philip, Mary Eleanor Ann,

There being no bastards, I can swear to it,
And Caspar dead without issue,
Dead and beyond amends, if they will pay my transit

The rest is theirs as they feared it would not be
When I was famous for my fondness for Caspar,
Everything theirs in perpetuity:

A maze, a thousand-year-old yew, a black carp pond,
Forty-four windows opening south
Over the Garden of Eden of England

Unless I dreamed it and the whole estate
Is this tin box I rest on in which are
His letters, his pretty paintings, a lock of his hair

I cut myself the day
I committed him into a tributary of the Acheron
That took him like a magnet and I turned away.

Famous Stanhopes are ten a penny. I
Wish the mark I have made on life were made
On rented sand a little above low tide

But I am shackled to a revenant,
I and that woman and the dim professor,
The chief of police, the parson and the mayor

And Stephanie the Duchess, all
In the yellow livery of betrayal
We tag along whenever Caspar walks.

They called my father Citizen. He swore
By the youthful dead at Valmy and Jemappes,
Wept like a widow over Thermidor

And when what rose at last out of the lake of blood
Was only an emperor's head
Citizen Stanhope returned to private life,

He laboured night and day at merciful inventions
But all his hopes were consigned to future generations,
To a new race, he said, one whom

The true republic would fit
Like the easy clothing of the Greeks. Till then:
Work, work. Us, his children,

Gazing ahead he entirely overlooked.
Nothing could come of us, born when we were
In dead time. We fled the centre.

Two were in Greece. Spencer
Got the topography of the Peloponnese by heart
Walking. He mapped Olympia. I sometimes thought

He would go down and down among the exhalations of the dead
Knee deep, chest deep, by degrees
Vanishing, and map Hades.

Leicester was more with the living at Missolonghi.
He said they would raise the temples again on a real ground
But sailed on the *Florida* from Zante

Home, with Byron's corpse. I was abroad somewhere,
Nowhere particular, when I read in a newspaper
Of my brother committing the poet to the grief of the nation.

If I can get any ship to ferry me
I shall berth quietly and keep
My grave like a man who knows he will not sleep

For Caspar calling. Famous
More or less crazy Stanhopes litter the earth.
Hester swelled in a ruined oasis

East of Palmyra like a queen bee
All day in bed smoking a foul black shag,
Men in her *ruelle*. Each with his swag

Everyone left her when she began to die.
They ran away down separate radii.
She lay at the empty centre, turning.

I made little sorties away from home
On the usual routes. Truth is
No sooner across the Channel I began to dream

I would be happier at my garret window
Staring down the dead straight drive to the Temple of Virtue
Or down the long diagonal across the deer park

To the wood all afternoon or leaned
Against the far wall of the nursery
Watching the door. No sooner abroad I dreamed

I was summoned home for a game of hide and seek
And went from room to room like a jovial father
Always calling so the child would never fear

He hid and no one sought and he might hide for ever
In a dark place and no one seek
And life close over him, but in my dream I spoke

A constant reassurance out loud
And the rooms brightened when I entered them
And I woke hearing the word 'welcome'.

Some evenings in a foreign language
In Baden, say, I hit the sickness for home
And my tongue ran on alone like the wheel of a crashed carriage.

Some nights I was visited by the pure ghost
Of thirst, but not for drink, and hunger, but not for food,
As though the poles pulled equally and the needle was denied

Even the relief of pointing. The trick is then
To spin a new thing as God did
In the space for Adam but Stanhope was a weak man

And soon swung to Chevening
And Lady Stanhope and the two children
And posted home, ignoring

Devils at either ear who whispered he would mate
Like a stupid bull with a counterfeit.
I lost heart the moment we entered the drive

Like blood from a slitted pig. The property
Faced me like the water, the leper
Or the five thousand had I

Impostured Christ. In the summer of 1829
Drifting among the princedoms vaguely south again
He read Caspar's dream of a stately home

As Daumer had made it public in the *Bavarian Courier*
And Feuerbach's note: that no dreamer
(Unless God) creates *ex nihilo*

But the flutes and vistas, the rides, the water-gardens
Must have seeded themselves long since
Through little apertures and feelers of sense

And survived a vanished childhood as seeds do
Ice and fire to flower now
In speech from the boy's mouth.

I was 47, slipping.
All I had in my favour was restlessness.
His dream of a home, only lodging,

Touched me, lodging, whose large estate
Whenever I came to feast on it with the five senses
Shrank and stiffened as though I sickened it.

I had resolved to kill myself at 50
But hoped God knew and would lean down
And stop me on the road with a clear sign

And reading Caspar's dream in an old journal
I thought that if it fitted my own grounds and rooms
At last some blood might vivify my phantoms

And I bore towards Nuremberg post haste,
Breaking an axle. The news there
Was all of his near-murder.

I queued with the common people on the island.
He was bandaged still. He raised his hand
Making a lorgnette of his thumb and finger.

A miniature: sunk eyes, thin lips,
The long Etruscan nose: impossible to tell
If what his Lordship wants inhabits heaven or hell.

II

I open easily. The eye,
Ringed like a burning glass, entered me without resistance.
I would have declared myself at once

And offered him Chevening for his dream
But suddenly blood showed
Through the white bandage and the mother shooed

Us out. We were three. I stood between
A butcher and a witch with a harelip
Who said the blood was a bad sign

And crossed herself. The butcher shrugged. I shook
Like a quaker then and let speak
What was in me, saying God has pointed, the little start of blood

Marks it and I gave my name, saying
Remember this, and the name of my house in Kent,
Saying remember this too and tell your children you were present

At the start. Tongues,
The French, the German, the Italian,
Came easily to Stanhope, he went headlong

Down the rapids of difficult constructions
An ace in the art but helpless so that his family lived in fear
Of what he would give some foreigner

His word on next. Below the nose
His face fell away in a small landslide
Which he raised a hand to hide

So that even speaking the heart's opinion
He seemed to defer and wish to burden
A listener only with a filtered truth.

He backed away. He considered flight to the frozen poles
Or Africa but trailed in spas and the little German capitals,
In the wings, within earshot. Lives appeared

And the first hostile pamphlet: CASPAR HAUSER
NOT IMPROBABLY AN IMPOSTER.
Stanhope paid his valet a bounty on every item.

Tall, uneasy in his clothes
(For years he wore green against all advice
So that they called him Grasshopper or the Praying Mantis)

He sent to Paris for a novelty in morning suits –
A Caspar Hauser – and stood in it
At fairs among the illiterate

Gawping at a Caspar raised high
On a banner in bright colours with his wide-awake hat
And heard the ballad of the wonderful boy

Sung by a hurdy-gurdy man, a dame
Teaching the people the stations of his life
To date, frame by frame

With a stick. He says: No stanzas
Ever went home into my heart like those.
Further, I saw him staged in five cities

As a clown, barefoot, matted,
He swam in the aquarium of my tears.
And yet it was half a year till I admitted

I was no freer than a petty moon.
Nuremberg sucked on me like the hole in a maelstrom
But I pulled away as far as Amsterdam

All the while knowing this: a peer
Of England with ten thousand a year
Being the big fish in Germany's small ponds,

Though nothing much to look at, if he muscles in
Who will resist the star, the gartar, the ermine
And drafts on ample funds in his thin hand?

Stanhope expects a decade off his time in purgatory
For every month he held
His person at a distance. Lord Chesterfield

(An uncle) challenged any man
To distinguish a long vain struggle against temptation
From the judicious deferment of a gratification.

Caspar was riding out with Clara Biberbach.
Her black gelding, his red mare,
The silver waistcoat he wore

Which she had sewn for him with ghostly poppies
Were known to everyone who read the newspapers.
The accident of 3rd April

Travelled like starlight to remote salons.
Caspar was rising like a drowned man
In the consciences of person or persons

Unknown, and Anselm Feuerbach
Was nailing him with facts to a family tree
But Stanhope mooching on the periphery

Collected evidence like a lovesick chambermaid:
Gossip and nonsense, playbills,
The first poor lithographs, the booktrade's

Beginning boom in Hauseriana –
He drew it all upon himself as though he were smeared
With honey and so martyred

By bees and ants. In Delft his hostess
Wondering would no one save the Child from wickedness
He felt God's finger on him

And rode at Nuremberg, but lost
Heart or found the strength to resist
And swerved to Teplitz, sending from there

A Present Help, (London 1828),
Being a Pharmacopeia of Prayers for a Soul Beset,
His own work, and a bare card:

A Friend. He waited. News came
Jostling through the news of the July Days
That Caspar, innocent as Joseph, was put out of house and home.

Stanhope thanked God for the efficacy
Of prayer, but dreamed that night he was kneeling with Clara
Before Caspar, and like the Celestial City

Chevening shone behind them. In Carlsbad
Exercising in a formal garden
Shoulder to shoulder, arm in arm, tête-à-tête

With nodding members of Old Europe
He heard it said for certain that Caspar Hauser,
The automatist, the idiot of Nuremberg, was heir

To the throne of the Grand Duchy of Baden
Being the child of Stephanie
Stolen from her still bloody

After a hard birth. And more:
That the righteous were arming themselves with proofs and power
To carry Caspar home in a rush of glory.

Stanhope vanished. His valet tracked him down
To poor lodgings on the German plain.
He lay curled like a hero on his sword

Or a green caterpillar, skewered
On jealousy. The whore Clara was nothing after all.
Mannheim was his rival:

A palace. He saw the illumination
Of every window in the House of Baden
And the veil of his own house rent in twain.

The year turned. He was becoming fifty.
He asked for a sign. None came. The resorts were empty.
He crossed and saw his home again in a bitter starlight.

Ice cave. The Master fled
And wintered in a priory near Dover. There
He thought a good deal about his dead father

The Citizen, and a large idea for the regeneration of Man
From a source in England (Chevening)
Through innocence (Caspar) ran

Wild in his head. He says:
I wrestled against my feeling of election
And lost. He sent his valet to purchase

The best grammar of the English tongue
And quitted his cell. He sniffed the sea and the spring.
A thousand happy devils were rollicking in his heart.

III

Pecca fortiter, says Luther. Do it, if you must,
Hard. Stanhope came on
Full, as an English gentleman,

But behind a handkerchief sidling away,
Drawing his listeners after him in a shuffling orbit
Around Caspar who stood as stiff as a spit

Rotating. They danced thus
In the drawing room of Jakob Friedrich Binder, Nuremberg's mayor.
Gottlieb von Tucher was there

As present custodian of the Child's virtue
After Clara. Stanhope,
Blushing, retreating, offered up

Thanks to God on behalf of the human race
For havens such as Gottlieb von Tucher's house
In a naughty world. Caspar was dumb but turned

His friendly beam on the green lord.
The Mayor, scenting money, encouraged them
Into the walled garden for a private word.

The policemen were at the gate, helmet to helmet,
The common people lined their heads along the coping
And every window craned over the stooping

Foreigner and the boy prised out of the earth
Three years since exactly whose small hands
Were good with horses and whose countenance

Ruddy enough to pass for one of ours
Carried the marks of the razor and the ball
And hoped for kindness like the fleece under the dewfall.

Everyone's breath drew in when Stanhope arrested
The boy's shoulder and read
His lifted face for a while, and when the walk continued

Caspar Hauser was clamped to a new patron
By a fatherly arm. So the town
Where he had landed saw him being taken

Off the books, a saving, off their hands and out of their lives,
A lightening, a grief.
The Earl laid a finger on his lips

And Caspar grinned. Something was on the child
No one quite liked when Stanhope
In the hearing of all of them who had called

Him theirs, said my –
My Caspar, my poor child, my dear boy –
And gave him a grammar and primer of the English tongue,

The speaking made easy. Lodged at the Blackie Boy
Stanhope sent for him out of a scripture lesson
To ride on the ramparts, luncheon

In a greenery, a stroll
With a long following, a farewell all
The polite and vulgar walkers halted to witness.

Five hundred gulden crossed from bank to bank.
We name no names, said the *Courier*,
But raise our hats. The Lord's long finger

Opening the fob slit in the waistcoat sewn
With pale poppies let slide
A gold watch into Caspar's side:

A plain face, time passing
No faster, of course, but with a quaker frankness.
How often we saw Caspar press

His left hand there, puzzled, as though
He were reminded of an old trouble
But could not put a name to it and when he drew

The timepiece out he looked like a conjuror
Who has amazed himself. But the way he wound the thing in public
As pompously as an alderman and listened to it tick

We said this is the corruption working. His first pleases
And thank-yous in the English tongue
Caused us to laugh behind our hands as would indecencies

Taught to a parrot. However
His meeting with Clara Biberbach cheered us somewhat.
She was walking alone, no one would speak to her,

In the Nuns' Garden, and he was arm in arm
With the long-nosed lord saluting the world
And when he saw the scarlet woman who had done him harm

It would be right to say that his face lit up
From within, from out of the core of his generous soul,
And from her face which we admit was beautiful

Light also fell and he smiled
Just so, like a field
When the sun comes suddenly. Taking her hand

And Stanhope's, the way he beamed
Icebergs would have melted
But not them, they repelled

Being like poles bent
Equally on Caspar, they stood off stiffly
Though he joined (we heard him say) present

And past kindness in their hands
Babbling until Milord with English courtesy
Cold as a gorgon gave her good-day

And pulled the harder. It was that afternoon
He paid for privacy at our bathing place,
Setting sentries, and went down

Under the eyes of the valet who held a towel
Naked into the pool
Hand in hand with the unbaptised Caspar.

But for his small hands and his face
Grown used to the sun how white he was
But for the one dark place

His parts inhabited like fledglings in a nest
How white was all the rest
So that I thought and thought of his years in the earth,

His unfired clay, the dough of him
Unready for eating like
The unrisen Lord stretched in the cromlech.

But as for swimming, he was more stone than fish
And I was obliged to buoy him, he lay
Face up on the palms of these same hands, he trusted me,

I whispered him into believing the miracle
He would float like a compass needle
On the water's skin. I spoke of sea-baths

And of dips at Chevening: how we ran, would run or would have run
As man and boy on my estate
Bare foot through the grey dew and the cuckoo-spit

And took the towel from my valet whose eyes were as cold as flint
And sent him to fetch some warmer covering
And I turned myself to Caspar who was shivering.

I towelled him dry as any father would. The wet
Lay on him in the sunshine like a night sweat
As I rose with my hand into the fork of him.

My valet clothed him in a tartan cloak.
Both watched me dress
Suddenly in a hurry over my nakedness

Fumbling and red, I made them turn away
And shook and wept by the quiet pool
For reasons I cannot name even today.

IV

Flights: the second
Was after the occasion at the bathing place
When the sentries opened

A path for the Earl, still dressing,
And Caspar in a tartan cloak
To the cushioned carriage. As though a snake

Were threading his vertebrae
Stanhope had long repercussions of the river's cold
For days, especially

Seeing Caspar, seeing down his stiff arms
Shock after shock of welcome travel
Into the proferred palms

And spiked fingers, each day, whenever he,
(His guardian angel, they had begun to say)
The Lord, appeared, it smiled

So without apprehension over Caspar's face
Most of us looked away
As from a thing we had no right to witness.

It was early June. The river's cold
Or some equivalent in the subterranean child
Shaking his Lordship daily like malaria

He announced a necessary absence throughout the summer
To recover vital heat
At spas, lying in sulphur,

And left money for tuition in English
And let it be known it was his wish
The boy should be addressed henceforward as My Lord

Adoption being very likely
Into the bosom of a fortune
And elevation to the rank of firstborn son

Who must embrace an undertaking
As large as Christ's
From his (the Baptist's)

Home. He fled
In wraps and furs on a broiling day
Yellow and ill. The people crossed themselves, they said

There goes the devil posting back to hell
And we assembled at the Blackie Boy
Where Caspar waited to be said goodbye.

I could not. Neither then
Nor when I left him last. I am the man
Who wrote a letter to the boy he loved

Knowing him dead
As though the letter might be forwarded
Knowing the Christmas snow

There in the little town I left him in
Was red for all to see
With scribbles nobody could understand but me.

❦

Fifth Canto

GEORG FRIEDRICH DAUMER
1 January 1875

I saw him last in the summer before he died.
August. He visited me. It was being said
His triumph was near. One of our kings,

De passage in Nuremberg, received him kindly.
The woman had gone by then, to France,
I believe. Good riddance,

Everybody said, seeing her poor children
And poorer man, but I said nothing for I had begun
To pity her. Caspar wept

There on the street below her windows
Seen by all, and hurried to find me on the island
And we had two days

Reprieve in the house and garden. Near my statue
Shutting his eyes he asked could he recite
An English prayer and when we ate

Would we excuse him meat. The river wreathing us,
I congratulated him on his recent confirmation
Exhaustively reported in our newspapers

And I saw him troubled
As he never was or could have been with me
And I wondered who had enabled

His innocence to this.
I said I knew his pastor for a decent man.
Caspar replied: Lord Stanhope wishes

Yourself particularly a long life
In better health and begs that you will think him
The honest friend of Caspar Hauser through thick and thin,

Blushing. He gave me lettters, a fat wad,
And I saw my name like an insect trapped
There in the netting of his Lordship's German script

And felt the cold again, remembering Feuerbach,
My comrade in the struggle for Caspar's good,
Dead at Whitsun, poisoned, leaving his book

Shoulder to shoulder with mine in a world of calumny
And I envied him
His tomb for its quiet and safety.

Caspar slept in the room of his convalescence.
I read the letters as he wished me to,
Hurting my eyes, the Englishman's

Too fluent reproduction of our tongue
And characters was like a skin
That something writhed and shone and postured in,

Something I will not put a name to even now
But say: a man whose mania
Was covering paper here let himself go

Over the white sheets of my Caspar's heart and soul
Scribbling and scribbling till the boy
So written over never would clarify

As a person should, from ferment. I was there,
Though ill, in November 1831
When Stanhope by the main force of his peerage won

Custody of Caspar out of the honest hands
Of Gottfried Christian von Tucher and left this town
More like a kidnapper than a guardian

Caspar waving through the carriage window
To me especially and to the woman who
Unveiled herself and showed a face so full of sorrow

Eyes were lidded. We had said
The fondness, the embraces and the kisses
Stanhope allowed the child exceeded what was right and witnesses,

Myself, though ill, among them, spoke against
His seizing. In vain.
I lay in the dark a week and heard the rain

And felt the river swell and let itself
Into the cellars of my house
And wash the rats on rafts from shelf to shelf

And land them on the steps. But then my book was out
With Anselm Feuerbach's in a brave tandem
Against the lies already taking root

And for a testimony of innocence
And preservation of our century's last chance.
In vain. My Caspar slept

Where we had laid him in the whitewashed room
After his wounding, safely, there
I had him safe still in my house and home

And never slept but wounded my weak eyes
Over the devil's close calligraphy until
Birds sang, light came and I resolved to seize

My life's last chance and his. The sun appeared
Thin and white. I stood in my garden
Like an eloper willing the windows of his room to open

On the sharp air. I sent
Mother in to wake him early. She was present
And Caroline too when I

At the end of the summer of 1833, his last,
Over the last meal he would eat with us,
Spoke with a young man's boldness

Astounding the women
To Caspar, my ward and pupil,
There breaking bread for the last time at our table

And drinking milk. Firm of purpose
I begged him to leave the servitude in Ansbach,
The waiting on an absent lord in a brutal house,

And leave the priests and their unnatural creed
For me, but not to come
Into the shelter of my moated home

There being none, no shelter, no asylum –
Witness the black
Ribbon I wore for Feuerbach –

But leave with me, leave house and home and town
And petty fatherland and walk
South, under other names, as teacher and pupil, down

The almost autumn roads and over the snow,
As pilgrims, going poor
For freedom and the mind's enlightenment and no

More dread. All this
Shielding my vision but in a steady voice,
With a young man's resolve. The women said

Your eyes. I answered:
The unclouded light and the long views will cure them or
Caspar will lead me. Your books, they said.

I answered that my books, except the last,
On Caspar, belonged in the stove, to stoke,
And nothing would come of me in Germany that woke

And lived but in the south it might,
A proper writing, a book fit to read,
About escape, about the soul's right

To life grasped firmly like a bowl of wine and drunk
Into the bloodstream, like bread
Ingested, to give heart and feed

Faith up when it lapses and we settle for less and less,
A book men who profess
To teach should write, or none,

Turning to Caspar. He sat
As though the sun on him were ice
Shivering, white, and little heads of sweat

Stippled his scars like leprosy.
Cannot, he said. And must not. He was bound
To wait in lodgings to be summoned

By messenger or till the guardian angel came
Whose mansion would be Caspar's for the rest of time
In person. He reached

The letters into a hiding place
Next his heart. Then all
My column of spirits fell

Into the cold bulb,
And the screaming began again out loud
Where we had hushed it and the stink of fear and the blood

Returned to the rooms we had aired
With fires and breezes and scoured
Nearly white and Caspar backed away

Past the privy and the trap door
His left hand pressing the lump of letters on his heart
His right warding me off as though I were

Incarnate death. And that was our goodbye:
My Caspar backing to the bridge
Stooping and crumpled under the sort of knowledge

Masks have uttered through their mouth-holes
And seen through empty eyes
In theatres in the crucibles of hills

Where men and women were cradled for the gods
To grind. He ran. I lay for days
Hearing the winds strip the big chestnut trees

And the rain come, sufficient rain
To sluice away a massacre. I rose to watch the snow
Whiten over everything around my house and in the town

And then came news of the red pocks,
The red script, the red desperate prints
Over the snow in Ansbach at the time of gifts and cribs

And the nativity of the innocent
Lamb. And see me now
In Bismarck's day, in Nuremberg, the snow

Descending calmly, knowing its resources,
Knowing the leaden heaven
Can snow for ever if it chooses

And cover everything. What Stanhope wished me
I had half of: the long life, outliving them all,
Sickly, behind the rising courses of my wall

Of books which I will cram the stove with
Faster and faster while the snow falls, and less
For warmth than to be rid of myself, to cease

Leaving nothing, since nothing
Has come of me but words and I am making
Smuts of writing still on another page.

I hope the snow falls, on and on,
After the ash of my own substance has fallen
And there is whiteness over the streets and parks

Only whiteness over the whole town
And on the whiteness, when I am dead,
No smuts of print or ink, no spots of blood.

Sixth Canto

PHILIP HENRY STANHOPE
1 March 1855

I read their books and grasped this:
That he was fading, the light
Off him, the magic in him was less and less

And I must rub him like a used charm,
Massage the heart and suck
Hard for the virtue sunk back

Towards his centre. I blamed God
To His face for not crossing
My line of life and the boy's at the beginning

That first Whit and letting
The Professor have him for a curiosity
And the corrupters touch him while I

Dawdled somewhere in Europe,
Nowhere particular, empty and my
Heart withering up

For want of the flood of grace. Fleeing
Again and again (like a man who
At last gets his hands on the last few

Sybilline pages and leaves those
Somewhere ridiculous where the wind blows
To rest his fitness to own them in the lap of merest chance)

I dreamed of Caspar as a vial of blood
But white, enshrined
At the very heart of my house in poor England

Pulsing, giving forth
Even through the body of the reliquary
Like a vast opal a power to ease the earth

Of every sin and affliction and when that dream came
I whined in terror, told his name
Over and over against the stacking odds,

Swung like a weather cock and thrust
At him again from a lodging on the edge.
Once I had got him in my tutelage

In Ansbach naturally
I reverted his diet to the vegetable.
In vain. Wherever the source lay we

Were far below, he wasted in the ordinary sun
Like the Ice King fetched down
From the glaciers into a dull town on the plain

And I blamed the Professor for not swaddling him
At once in something impermeable
And letting the wicked and the social

Crowd leach him. So he withdrew
As would the face on the Turin shroud
If we hung it merely as a curtain at our window

And the clever jurist drawing a family tree
Of dead branches, rotten fruit
And a trunk as stabbed and scabbed and poxy

As any in Europe was all astray
And only made a beam and a gallows tree
To crucify him on. Fool

Having understood
The offence was the killing of a childhood
And the injured party the soul itself

Then to pursue the poor requital in their gift
And reinstatement into their charnel house
As though you graft

The mercifully severed one good hope
Back on disease. I would
Have carried him into my desert like Aaron's rod

And rammed him home there
Where it was fittest he should flower
For all our good. My children stopped me in a Baltic port

And wrestled with Satan for my soul, they said.
My flesh, more like. Ten thousand pounds
A year of it. But I had promised God

To rescue Caspar out of the Cities of the Plain
And fetch him into the mountains
And live among simple people, beginning again

The crippled trek away from our damnation. But I slipped
Down from my fastening on his outstretched arms
Down and wept

And swallowed gall and wormwood like the Madalene
And see his face still, flat and blank as the moon,
Not exactly smiling, rather frozen

Into an expression not of his own making,
A sort of smile, but too preoccupied
With its own puzzle, the eyes too wide

And blind to smile on me. So I have lived
Year after year and watched him rise
Nightly over the edge into my cold skies

And hang there puzzling and afraid
And never once incline his face to me
However I begged. He bowed

His head last when I asked him to
When I was leaving, let it fall abruptly
As though my asking him withdrew

His ownership. I cut
A lock of hair off with my nail scissors
And pocketed it.

❦

Seventh Canto

GEORG FRIEDRICH DAUMER
1 January 1875

I read their books and I know this:
He died badly, they were gathered round,
Meyer the brute, the decent pastor, the whole crowd,

Hoping for words such as he spoke
To Mother, Caroline and myself
When the Visitor bled him and it woke

His powers again, but all
That issued from his mouth was babble
Of wrong and horror. The pastor grieved

But it was so. There stood
Taller than any others at his bed
Something he never took his eyes off and called

Monstrous, the monster, that word showed
Like the hand or face of a man drowning
Time and again in his flood

Of tongues. And this:
Too strong, the monster, too big, too many hands it has.
And also this: Let my Lord Stanhope

Guard against evil. And again:
Monster, monstrous. And I have it for certain
What drew the child just come of age

To the monument was Stanhope's name
And the promise of news
Of him, lodged, spider or fly, who knows,

In the outer web. Late afternoon
And barely lit by snow
Already crisping, the families gone down

Into the streets and homes
Only the birds left fretting
When a park becomes

As chilling for a town to contemplate
As the gaps in constellations
Caspar entered, hurrying. No one's

Face ever lifted as his did on a hope of welcome
Nor heart opened and often
I called him only for that reason

To see his face and saw
In the measure of his joy how far below
His heart's deserts I fell and so

Uplifted
Whoever called him away from the lighting lamps
Saw him, and slid

Into the opening between
Rib and fob an icicle
Whose watermark was the hour glass and the skull

And saw his simple expectation of a kindness
Curdle to something more
Suited to the truth of us: terror.

When the snow was gone and with it the blood in the spring rain
And Caspar had a tomb
As safe as houses his Lordship came

In a sweat to Nuremberg, seeking me out.
I would not receive him on the island in my house
But answered at the Blackie Boy. Is it thus

We shall appear for ever under Caspar's eyes:
Yellow, unable to sit still?
The man spoke pell-mell

And always through his handkerchief as though his breath
Stank, which it did if by the breath
We mean how the soul breathes

For Stanhope's soul had died
And against the stench of it rotting he had need
Of more than a hand and a handkerchief.

He said he hoped I lived safely
And nothing worse than voices would be raised against me
And never an arm fitted with a cutting edge

And best to err, for the sake of my womenfolk,
On the side of the new truth
And this (suddenly, with a bare mouth,

And starting eyes as though he shocked himself):
Whatever we say it cannot hurt him now.
There was a diary. We knew

His Lordship had sacked the Meyers' house from cellar to attic
And opened the belly of Caspar's stove to sift and weigh
The delicate leaves of his last auto-da-fé

But could read nothing. He feared
My heart, having beat with Caspar's a last time,
Might be the repository of some gloss on the word

Monstrous, which by then
Was known in every salon as the burden
Caspar dragged with him through his agony.

We faced each other across a common table.
His Lordship looked to be already burning
In ice, which strengthened me. Next morning

Sleepless, my eyes as sore
As cockscombs, I had in mind to stick him to the door
With questions, but found him breakfasting

On meats: on kidneys, livers and a sheep's heart
And rare steaks as fat
As policemen's soles. I stood, he ate,

He fed some hunger in him far down,
Watching me, and never spoke and fed
On meat that dribbled red,

Kidneys that spurted, a flecked liver,
A slop of lights and all the while
He eyed me as though I might contest the spoil

Or like a man caught itching at a vicious place
In public but cannot stop, though watched,
And grubs for easement, he scratched

At the sore of his hunger as if to say
See me, stare at me, see how it is
At the feeding time of the worm in me

And drank the juices off his silver plate and mopped
It clean as a child's brow and drained
A black wine after it and swabbed

His lips with a snowy cloth
And never spoke, only stared at me, and I withdrew
And on the street there in the public view

Vomited and lay
Curled and retching on a point of bile,
The people torn between that spectacle

And Stanhope's flight. My friend
And physician Dr Osterhausen being summoned
Failed to unclench me and I was borne

Rolled like a grub into my sanctuary
That stank of blood and howled
From cellar to attic for the absent child.

Eighth Canto

We never sleep. We have no empty squares.
It would be impossible to deliver him
So he stood out. The wars

Blow children up. Some fall our way.
They know a single sentence. They can say
My father is dead in somewhere in the news,

My mother raped and dead, or thrust it down
In somebody else's lettering
Over our headlines in the underground,

Or howl, just that: a particular girl
Rides the loop, stop by stop,
And holds a stump out and a begging cup

And howls, just that. I have observed her eyes.
They are so absent you would say she hires
Herself as a professional keener in her cause.

And nobody looks at anyone else, we all
Pray there'll be no hold-up for the howl
Cannot be borne beyond its usual

Measure. And much the same
Like wreckage after a catastrophe we have not fathomed yet
Children of our own making squat

Along the concrete walkways and the bridges
We cross to the opera
And hold a cardboard in their laps that says

What their state is. And not long since
At the time of the clear-outs and the big shut-downs
The insane appeared among us in great numbers,

They collected steadily like a bloom
And had to be dispersed. We called them
The big children, the way they lumbered,

Also because they were taking it up again –
Life, I mean –
After a long time hidden

Under the stairs, in cubby-holes, behind the door
Playing hide and seek
And nobody seeking, so three score

Had to be stiched back on to the ten
Or less, which made a shadow
Far too heavy for a child to tow.

Most were as delicate,
Faint and intricate
As snowflakes when they land too soon

On the unhushed concrete or press
At the warm pane of a living room
And with very little fuss

They expired somewhere. Round here
I believe King Billy is the only survivor.
The Pakistanis took him in, to sweep,

And lately they have let him mind the children.
He has a lizard's eyes and a lizard's skin.
It might be several lifetimes

He lived elsewhere before he was returned to us,
The community, his neck cricked
As from a failed hanging, and the head thus cocked

As if he were always listening, which he is
Since everyone coming out had his particular voices
For guidance how to get on

In the increased traffic. But King Billy hears
The languages of all the nations he will rule one day
In peace, from Sans Souci.

Each new one heard he learns
Until his conversation with the voices is word perfect.
He is above dialect.

He learns the mandarin. This purity
Shines out in the children's
English and Hindi. You will say

Town is crawling with men who think they are Jesus
Or Winston Churchill and accost the public
With proofs, in bus stations. King Billy never does

But keeps his council. He has waited so long
There are so many tongues
The grammars of some are hard to get

And the good forms almost forgotten. Hospitals
Were razed and rose again over him like cathedrals
Over an ancient crypt

Where he bowed and studied. He has time on his side.
His eyes are as lasting as diamonds, his bald head
Looks to have lifted clear of the pool of aging.

He says he was put away for safekeeping
Until the fires have passed. It moves me
That he does not think he has come out too early.

He stands at the zebra between
Two bright-as-a-button Paki kids, their hands
Trusting in his, he waits for green

On a street still wearing the black of arson
And will tell you in any language, if you ask,
The time will come. Then I imagine

Caspar entering down the long road
From the upland fields through the plots
Of sunk endeavour and the walled estates

His stride made for him by the man behind with kicks
Like someone carrying a carapace
Already smashed towards a starting place

Under the neon in the whiff of drains
Against an aureole of shattered plate
In the racket of jackpots, the sirens,

The shots, the mirth, the fires
As nightly. But other pairs
Compete. Bone comes in

Pick-a-back
Knotted around the midriff and the neck
Of Dai, his pal, with equal arms and legs

And lately I have watched a mother and son
Put out, invade
Again and again down the same road

Like damp. She wheels him in
Wrapped like her grandfather, they suck the same bottle
Over his shoulder to and fro, their purple

Blustering faces bear
Less a family likeness than the common
Look of matter in decomposition

Wherever it shows
Cakey and fissuring. She vents herself, she slews
Him off the edge, he tips and bleeds.

Hard to be noticed in a town like this,
Even the double acts. Day in, day out
A grown man stands with a bible on the martyrs' spot

And bellows at the traffic. No one hears.
It rains. He wags his book and roars
And no one listens. True,

Anyone dying in a pyre still makes the news
But no one rightly knows
What they should do about him doing it.

Whether to look. The police advise
Against it. Eyes
Often are only waiting for that contact

To strike you dead. Best look away,
Look down, chasten
Your wanton eyesight like a nun

Since any beggar or whore
Whose mouths are asking you to give or buy
Their eyes want more.

Prostitution in a cold climate
Sad, the heels
In dirty puddles

The stockings in a wind
Sharp as cystitis. When the silvery captains land
From taxis, bible-black, the hand,

French or the full supper
Is theirs in the minutes before departure
For next to nothing. All these children

God knows what maladies riding their veins
The way they look at you over their captions
The way they look at you over their mouths

Worse than Christ at the whipping-post who knew
The answers, they ask questions worse
Than what is this and what am I to you,

Stranger, passer-by? They ask
What am I to me? And nobody knows.
They seem to have moved out into their own shadows

And sit watching their bodies round
Over a bowl or tin at the level of our footsteps.
Last night this happened:

I stooped to give a coin, he caught my wrist
As though I thieved, he raised
His look under my guard

And we opened, both, the need, the helplessness,
The infinite requirement of redress,
We admitted them, he appeared

Like the moon in the dish of a telescope
Fetched into perfect focus, near
As the lines of life on my own palm, but deep

In space circling
The warmer life in a cold outer track
Presumably for ever. At my back

My fellow citizens were pounding to and fro
For trains, in the corridors, and he held me out of them
A minute perhaps, he held me to

The sight of him and cocked an ear
To signal me to listen to what it sounds like
Orbiting in the cold, what music they hear

Remote from one another: the whine of the last trains,
Their ghostly doubling in the underground winds,
These are cosy: it sounds

Like falling through eternity,
It is one steady incapable of ceasing,
Diminishing or commingling

Scream. When he was certain I had heard it
A little, and when he knew I knew
A little, he shrugged and let me go.

Tinkle of brass. I should have had him home.
Like Russian dolls, somewhere inside
The last would be the pale curled seed

Of him. Begin again.
He would be still there if I ever went that way.
I don't. He frightens me.

Best never look. I hear the scream
Most nights. I see his bit of card: to whom
It may concern. I read my name.

Ninth Canto

I

The College congregated
As they were required to when the case was special
All nine, some from a distance. He waited.

They kept him waiting in their coldest antechamber,
The ice house, a low
Tumulus in the snow

Outside the walls. One night, one day, one last night
The people queued to see him without distinction,
The dying wrapped tight,

The newborn and their mothers still unchurched,
Lovers, drunks, cretins, all ranks of these,
They queued to see him in the ice house.

The policeman at the entrance was unnecessary.
Nobody chattered until afterwards.
All stooped and entered with a perfect decency.

For so many years in the dark and the silence
When sleep was the only one who visited
Bringing him water and the carraway bread

After that prelude, after the morsel
Served him next, this coda: the people
Calling on him in their Sunday clothes

Two long nights and a brief winter's day
In the igloo where he lay
On a trestle table among candles

Only to see him with their own eyes
And never a word, a sigh perhaps, the shiver
Lines of verse will give but never

A word on him until they were home again
Somewhere warmer, thawing. Time had slowed
Almost to a halt in him, as when

He lived alone with the wheeled horses
And nothing happened but the kindnesses
Of sleep and all he did was host the nourishment

Through him and pet the horses while he grew
Only because flesh must
And never sleeps so deep it comes to rest.

Now in a sort of hive devised to thwart
The wish of ice in summer to become water
He hesitated and the College would have had him

As fresh as a visible mariner under the Pole
But that the candle tongues, the breaths of his visitors,
Their sighing, the condensation of their prayers

Warmed him a little as we have
The horses at Lascaux. So he had begun
To mottle slightly when the Academy called him in

And he was fetched through the people loath to see him go
To the steps and the doric portico
Where the Nine waited, in black, on high,

Each with his saws and knives in a black bag
Clutched like chastity
Under the paunch, unsmiling, whiskery

And red as diners. They bowed
And a murmur of grief rose from the ignorant crowd
And the beginnings of a mutter of complaint

When the beetle-black frock coats
Of the nine surgeons and the Academy's iron gates
And double iron doors closed on Caspar.

II

In there they got down to it
In shirt sleeves, tutting at
The greenish flecks of the life lived underground

Already advanced over the body of him
Who was as white as bread laid on their board
And scarcely cut. They heard

Schinder, the local man, tell yet again
How he was first and had laid an ear
On Caspar's chest and listened in

To the heart plashing like Daumer's rats
And with the middle finger of his right hand
Had gone as far as he could into the wound

And tickled what he thought was a wet lung.
When he was done, allowing
Themselves a pleasantry about this quizzy finger,

They fell to, the Nine, not like hyenas
On a unicorn, nor like
Crabs on a pearly mermaid, but as

Order dictated and the elbow room
Allowed. Off the breastbone
They laid the waistcoat of Caspar's flesh entirely open

And entered the zones of his wound from the right side
Sawing through the bars. He would have died
Four times had he had lives to do so:

Stomach, diaphragm, liver were all mortally hurt
In passing and the long finger of knife,
Its manicured long nail, had touched his heart

Whose sack had filled,
Likewise the thorax, likewise the abdomen,
Their sacks were full and on

Enquiry broke
Their septic waters over the ungloved hands
In pints. The heart was caked a thick

Yellow white
Like a baby and everywhere they went
Was soft and rank, in handfuls. But they lifted out

The spitted liver, rinsed it clean
And laid it for inspection on a silver dish.
It was the largest human liver they had ever seen.

So behind bars
The ape's grows and the bear's
And any wild thing's, out of all proportion, and in this,

Measuring the liver, they had gone beyond
The interrogation of the wound
Whose cause and effect were simple

And pushed their science
Into the enigma itself. Kratz took a leg
To a side table and dug

For the motor oddity. The organs
Of generation fell to Osterhausen
Who botched the job and every important question

Eluded him. The hands
That were quick and careful at drawing fruit and flowers
Did not detain them and they bent their minds

Over Caspar's face. He wore the angel's mark
And the mark of the accident
In Clara's house. Otherwise puzzlement –

That was how he had set and would have faded
Little by little had he been allowed
Time under a shroud –

Puzzlement settling finally into dust,
No bad ending, not a bad expression
To wear into extinction.

But the College, time pressing,
Time stoked by their hot breath accelerating,
Five hours in and the work of their hands stinking,

They wished to see behind the mere appearance
Behind the smile that was not exactly that
Behind the eyes that asked more than they answered.

Open as it always was still Caspar's face
Could not admit them without increase
Of routes. Schlott did a harsh caesarean on

The Child's skull
And proffered them the brain:
More beast than human, or if human

Only a foetus, untimely, the cerebellum
Too large for so ungrown a cerebrum,
The hind lobes scarcely started, the middle

Queerly sunk behind the sphenoid bone
As though reluctant. They sliced
The great brain flat, the smaller down

And there, in the latter, flowering like frost,
The wondrous spread of Caspar's *arbor vitae*,
Astonished them. The rest

Slicing and fingering they could make nothing of
And suddenly wearied. They saw
The stains on one another.

Kratz fetched the leg. Poor Osterhausen put
His parcel back. They shut
The skull over its infant brain and bedded

The liver in its morass. But for
What had run off and the few small
Souvenirs it was traditional

To abstract, they had
The makings of a person on their slab.
Dumb offal, reeking. Wetzel said:

We should have had him the minute he came out.
So much was blurred in the fatal interim
By a social life. We should have had him

Pure. They rang for the baggers and went to wash.
Late afternoon, already dark, more snow.
The men came, masked. One took a toe,

Another an ear, etc. They bagged up what remained.
After the obsequies – his pastor
Lifted the congregation on a swell of grief and terror –

The trade in him began, the entity,
Such as it was, the unsure
First person singular crumbling rapidly

He fed through the academies and the common people
Into the wide world, changing hands
For money one day, love the next, in lands

Only discovered since. Collected up
The crumbs still lodging here and there would make
More bread of life than Caspar ever broke.

❦

ALSO BY DAVID CONSTANTINE

SELECTED POEMS

POETRY BOOK SOCIETY RECOMMENDATION

David Constantine's *Selected Poems* includes a large selection of new work, as well as poems from his three previous collections *A Brightness to Cast Shadows*, *Watching for Dolphins* and *Madder*.

'Constantine has a generous, self-aware sensuality which he can express in a dazzling variety of tones on a wide variety of themes... His particular gift is for the reworking of classical myth and Biblical narratives so that they are infused with ordinary, accessible emotion and a sense of rich, humane acceptance' – FLEUR ADCOCK & MARINA WARNER, *Alice Hunt Bartlett Prize commendation*.

'*A Brightness to Cast Shadows* uses an impassioned, skilful lyricism to clarify a vision of experience that is both light and dark: love is affirmed, yet social wretchedness is treated with straightforward tenderness and Brechtian irony. *Watching for Dolphins* demonstrates a poignant obsession with loss and longing, often revivifying traditional myth. *Madder* is written in a leaner, seriously playful style that is responsive both to the sombre "noise / And shadow" of history and to the "manifest beauty of breathing"' – MICHAEL O'NEILL, *Oxford Companion to Twentieth-Century Poetry*

'Constantine's imagination moves gracefully within the classical precincts of the pure lyric, a Gravesian Muse poetry tempered with scholarship...intricate sensuality and an honesty of purpose that is impressive' – GEORGE SZIRTES, *The Literary Review*

'Constantine celebrates erotic experience in verse sentences of almost Jamesian intricacy and poise' – ROGER GARFITT, *TLS*

'His shimmering and classical illuminations fall with such intensity and conviction and his denunciations with such power and delicacy that I have no hesitation in placing him, thematically and formally, within the great Dantesque tradition' – DAVID ANNWN, *Anglo-Welsh Review*

Paperback: ISBN 1 85224 166 7   £7.95

DAVIES

A NOVEL

Davies was famous for a moment in 1911 when Home Secretary Winston Churchill raised his case in the House of Commons. But who was Davies? In this fictionalised account of a lifelong petty criminal, David Constantine unravels the mystery of a shadowy loner caught in a vicious circle of self-perpetuating crime.

David Davies (1849-1929) was known in his day as the 'Dartmoor Shepherd'. He spent half a century in prison for a succession of minor offences, mostly for stealing coppers from the poor boxes of local churches.

Davies came from Llanfyllin, Montgomeryshire, and Constantine has set his novel in the counties of the Welsh Marches. He has made much use of documentary material – Hansard, newspaper reports and a biography – and aims in his novel to seek a truth behind established facts. Although historically based, *Davies* is a novel whose concerns are very much relevant to the present day, particularly in its portrayal of the habitual offender and of vagrancy.

'*Davies* is a remarkable achievement, and not least for its bitter frugality of style…Constantine pieces Davies together from mist and myth, godly persecution and tolerance…The result is absorbing and disturbing' – CHRISTOPHER WORDSWORTH, *Guardian*

'The poet David Constantine speaks up for the socially edged-out …In *Davies*, Constantine's spare bare-knuckle prose makes marvellously present the harsh existence of his hero'
– VALENTINE CUNNINGHAM, *Observer*

'Constantine's unabashed seriousness has marked him out as a very European writer – an impression confirmed by his first novel *Davies*, which, with its documentary neutrality of tone and muted outrage at injustice, recalls, for example, the Böll of *The Lost Honour of Katharina Blum* much more than any contemporary British novelist's work' – TIM DOOLEY, *Times Literary Supplement*

Hardback: ISBN 0 906427 91 6   £7.95

Friedrich Hölderlin
SELECTED POEMS

TRANSLATED BY DAVID CONSTANTINE

Friedrich Hölderlin (1770-1843) was one of Europe's greatest poets.
The strange and beautiful language of his late poems is recreated in
English by David Constantine in these remarkable verse translations.

'Hölderlin is a poet we can read with our atrocious times in mind.
He is a deeply religious poet whose fundamental tenet is absence and
the threat of meaninglessness. He confronted hopelessness as few
writers have, he was what Rilke called 'exposed'; but there is no
poetry like his for the constant engendering of hope, for the ex-
pression, in the body and breath of poems, of the best and most
passionate aspirations' – DAVID CONSTANTINE

'Hölderlin's tragic life has become, in Keats's phrase, 'intrinsically
figurative'. We too easily see him as an archetype: the marginalised
visionary in an age of mercantile philistinism. The poems, on the
other hand, are more elusive. Their religious intensity and their
classical framework, their density and their verse forms all run out-
side the major English traditions. His poetic world is one of fracture,
absence and loss. The long central poem 'The Archipelago' offers
a terrible vision of the human condition. Set against this darkness,
however, is the brilliance of the ideal, which for Hölderlin found its
most absolute manifestation in Ancient Greece. The memory of this
perfection is at once our salvation and our grief, for it reminds us
of our loss and yet engenders a longing for future renewal...

'Along with lucid, informative notes, the selection contains an
excellent biographical introduction. There the reader is pointed to-
wards Michael Hamburger's monumental translation of Hölderlin's
work...Constantine allows himself more freedom and goes for an
'equivalence of spirit' in a more familiar idiom. This is at once a bold
and a humble undertaking, and has produced poetry of a remarkable
luminosity and intensity, written in rhythms and cadences which
recreate, both in their extremities of grief and their urgent hope,
the immediacy of the original' – KAREN LEEDER, *Oxford Poetry*

Paperback: ISBN 1 85224 064 4   £6.95

Henri Michaux
SPACED, DISPLACED
Déplacements Dégagements

TRANSLATED BY DAVID & HELEN CONSTANTINE
INTRODUCTION BY PETER BROOME

Henri Michaux (1899-1984) is one of the notable travellers of modern French poetry: not only to the Amazon and the Far East, but into the strange hinterland of his own inner space, the surprises and shocks of which he has never ceased to explore as a foreign country in their own right, and a language to be learned. Fired by the same explorer's appetite, he has delved into the realm of mescaline and other drugs, and his wartime poetry, part of a private "resistance" movement of extraordinary density and energy, has advertised his view of the poetic act as a form of exorcism.

His insatiable thirst for new artistic expressions of himself made him one of the most aggressive and disquieting of contemporary French painters. If he is close to anyone, it is to Klee and Pollock, but he was as much inspired by Oriental graphic arts.

Déplacements Dégagements (1985) has all the hallmarks of Michaux's most dynamic work: poetry testing itself dangerously at the frontiers, acutely analytical, linguistically versatile and full of surprising insights into previously undiscovered movements of the mind.

Helen Constantine has taught French at schools and polytechnics in Durham and Oxford. **Peter Broome** is Professor of French at Queen's University, Belfast. He is co-author of *The Appreciation of Modern French Poetry* and *An Anthology of Modern French Poetry* (CUP, 1976), and author of monographs on Michaux and Frénaud.

Paperback: ISBN 1 85224 135 7   £7.95

Philippe Jaccottet
UNDER CLOUDED SKIES / BEAUREGARD
Pensées sous les nuages / Beauregard

TRANSLATED BY MARK TREHARNE & DAVID CONSTANTINE
INTRODUCTION BY MARK TREHARNE

Poetry Book Society Recommended Translation

Philippe Jaccottet's poetry is meditative, immediate and sensuous. It is rooted in the Drôme region of south-east France, which gives it a rich sense of place. This book brings together his reflections on landscape in the prose pieces of *Beauregard* (1981) and in the poems of *Under Clouded Skies* (1983), two thematically linked collections which are remarkable for their lyrical restraint and quiet power.

Jaccottet's poetry is largely grounded in landscape and the visual world, pursuing an anxious and persistent questioning of natural signs, meticulously conveyed in a syntax of great inventiveness. His work is animated by a fascination with the visible world from which he translates visual objects into verbal images and ultimately into figures of language. His poems are highly attentive, pushing the eye beyond what it sees, enacting a rich hesitation between meaning conferred and meaning withheld.

Born in Switzerland in 1925, Philippe Jaccottet is one of the most prominent figures of the immediate post-war generation of French poets. He has lived in France since 1953, working as a translator and freelance writer. As well as poetry, he has published prose writings, notebooks and critical essays. He is particularly well-known as a translator from German (Musil, Rilke, Mann, Hölderlin) but has also translated Homer, Plato, Ungaretti, Montale, Góngora and Mandelstam. He has won many distinguished prizes for his work both in France and elsewhere. His *Selected Poems*, translated by Derek Mahon, was published by Penguin in 1988.

Mark Treharne taught French at the University of Warwick until 1992. He has translated much of Jaccottet's prose and written on modern French Literature. The translators worked in close collaboration with Philippe Jaccottet on this edition.

Paperback: ISBN 1 85224 184 5   £8.95

David Constantine was born in 1944 in Salford, Lancashire. He read Modern Languages at Wadham College, Oxford, and from 1969 to 1981 was a lecturer in German at Durham University. He is now Fellow in German at the Queen's College, Oxford. He is married with two children, and lives in Oxford.

His first book of poems, *A Brightness to Cast Shadows* (Bloodaxe Books, 1980), was widely acclaimed. His second collection, *Watching for Dolphins* (Bloodaxe Books, 1983), won the 1984 Alice Hunt Bartlett Prize, and his academic study, *Early Greek Travellers and the Hellenic Ideal* (Cambridge University Press, 1984), won the first Runciman Prize in 1985. His first novel, *Davies*, was published by Bloodaxe in 1985. His third collection, *Madder* (Bloodaxe Books, 1987), a Poetry Book Society Recommendation, won the Southern Arts Literature Prize. The French edition of *Madder*, translated by Yves Bichet as *Sorlingues* (Éditions La Dogana, 1992), won the Prix Rhône-Alpes du Livre. His *Selected Poems* (Bloodaxe Books, 1991) is a Poetry Book Society Recommendation. His latest books are *Caspar Hauser: a poem in nine cantos* (Bloodaxe Books, 1994), and *Back at the Spike* (Ryburn Publishing, 1994), his first book of short stories.

His other books include a critical introduction to the poetry of Friedrich Hölderlin (Oxford University Press, 1988), a translation of Hölderlin's *Selected Poems* (Bloodaxe Books, 1990), and a translation of Goethe's novel Elective Affinities (Oxford University Press, World's Classics, 1994). The Bloodaxe Contemporary French Poets series includes his translations of (with Helen Constantine) *Spaced, Displaced* by Henri Michaux (1992) and (with Mark Treharne) *Under Clouded Skies / Beauregard* by Philippe Jaccottet (1994).